USING
THIS
BOOK

*Children learn to read by* **reading**, *but they need help to begin with.*

**When you have read the story** *on the left-hand pages aloud to the child, go back to the beginning of the book and look at the pictures together.*

*Encourage children to read the sentences under the pictures. If they don't know a word, give them a chance to 'guess' what it is from the illustrations, before telling them.*

There are more suggestions for helping children to learn to read in the *Parent/Teacher* booklet.

---

**Note:** *In this story, there are several opportunities to discuss the best way of caring for wild creatures and pets.*

---

British Library Cataloguing in Publication Data

McCullagh, Sheila K.
    Peter Puffle's mouse. — (Puddle Lane. Stage 3; 7).
    1. Readers — 1950-
    I. Title    II. Morris, Tony, (date)    III. Series
    428.6    PE1119
    ISBN 0-7214-0962-8

First edition

Published by Ladybird Books Ltd Loughborough Leicestershire UK
Ladybird Books Inc Lewiston Maine 04240 USA

Printed in England

# Peter Puffle's mouse

written *by* SHEILA McCULLAGH
illustrated *by* TONY MORRIS

This book belongs to:

Ladybird Books

It was a very fine day.
The sun was shining down
on Puddle Lane, and
Davy and Sarah went out to play.
They were just going into the garden
at the end of the lane,
when they saw Peter Puffle.
"Sarah! Davy! Wait for me!"
shouted Peter Puffle.

Davy and Sarah were going
into the garden.
They saw Peter Puffle.

Peter was carrying a little cage,
with a white mouse in it.
"Just look at her!" cried Peter,
holding up the cage.
"Isn't she a beauty?"

"Don't make such a noise,"
said Sarah. "You'll frighten her."

"Where did you get her?" asked Davy.

"Uncle Percy gave her to me,"
said Peter Puffle.

Peter Puffle
had a little white mouse.

They went into the garden.
"I'm going to get some dry grass
for my mouse," said Peter.
"Then she can make a nest."

"We've got some nuts for the wood mice
who live in the hollow tree,"
said Davy. "Come and see them."

"They won't be as good
as my mouse," said Peter Puffle.
"She's the best mouse in Candletown."

They all went
into the garden
to get some grass
for the mouse.

As they went towards the hollow tree,
they saw Mr Gotobed.
Mr Gotobed was sitting on the grass,
propped up against a stone bench.
He was fast asleep.
"What's he sleeping there for?" asked Peter.

"He's always sleeping," said Sarah.

They saw Mr Gotobed.
"Mr Gotobed is always sleeping,"
said Sarah.

They came to the hollow tree.

"This is where the wood mice live,"
said Sarah.

"Have you got the nuts, Davy?"

Davy dropped a nut
into the hollow tree.

"I can't see any mice," said Peter.

"Sh!" said Sarah. "You'll frighten them."

The wood mice lived
in the hollow tree.
Davy dropped a nut
into the tree.

A wood mouse came out of a hole,
and began to eat the nut.
"Look!" cried Peter. "There's one!"
The wood mouse picked up the nut
and ran back down the hole.

"You've frightened him away,"
said Sarah. "You have to be quiet,
if you want to see wood mice."

"I'd rather have my mouse,"
said Peter. "She doesn't run away."

"She would if she could," said Sarah.

"No, she wouldn't," said Peter.

"Let's get the dry grass for her,"
said Davy.

A wood mouse came out
and ate the nut.
"Look!" cried Peter Puffle.
The mouse ran away.

There was some dry grass
by the hollow tree.
Some of it was very long.
Davy and Peter picked some handfuls
of dry grass.
As they went back towards the gates,
they passed Mr Gotobed.
Mr Gotobed was still fast asleep.
He was snoring gently.
Peter put down the grass, and
the cage with the mouse inside it.
"Watch me!" he said.

Mr Gotobed
was fast asleep.

He took a piece of long grass.
He tiptoed over to Mr Gotobed, and
began to tickle Mr Gotobed's nose
with the end of the grass.
Mr Gotobed's nose twitched.
Mr Gotobed brushed his hand across his face,
but he didn't open his eyes.

Peter Puffle tickled
Mr Gotobed's nose.
Mr Gotobed
didn't wake up.

Peter tickled Mr Gotobed's nose again.

Mr Gotobed shook his head,

but he didn't wake up.

Peter went on tickling.

Mr Gotobed gave a great sneeze.

**Atishoo!**

He opened his eyes, and sat up.

Peter hid the grass behind his back.

Peter Puffle tickled
Mr Gotobed's nose.
Mr Gotobed woke up.

"Hello, Peter," said Mr Gotobed.
"Are you playing in the garden?
There are a lot of flies
in here today. One of them
keeps landing on my nose!"
Mr Gotobed was just settling down
to go to sleep again,
when Sarah called out,
"Peter! Where's your mouse?
She's not in the cage."

Mr Gotobed
went back to sleep.
Sarah cried, "Look!"

Peter ran over to the cage.
The cage was empty.
The door was open, and
the mouse had gone.
"You let it out!" cried Peter.

"Of course I didn't," said Sarah.
"You must have knocked the
catch off the door,
when you put the cage down."
Peter began to cry.
"I've got to find her!" he said.

"We'll help you," said Davy.
"She can't have gone far."

"But you'll have to keep quiet,
Peter, or you'll frighten her,"
said Sarah.

The door of the cage
was open.
The little mouse
had gone.

They began to look for the mouse.

"What's that?" whispered Davy.

"Look — over there in the grass."

They crept over to look, but
it wasn't the mouse.

It was a frog.

"Where's it going?" whispered Davy.

"There's a lake on the other side
of the house," whispered Sarah.
"Perhaps it's going there."

"I've got to find my mouse,"
said Peter tearfully.

They looked for the mouse.
They saw a frog, but
they didn't see the mouse.

"Let's look along the wall," said Sarah.
"There are some holes there.
Perhaps she's gone into one."
There were some snails on the wall,
but there was no sign
of the mouse.

They looked for the mouse.
They saw the snails, but
they didn't see the mouse.

"She's not here," said Peter,
"and I've got to find her.
She must be **somewhere**."

"Perhaps she's with the wood mice,"
said Davy. "I expect she was lonely,
all on her own."

They were just going back
to the hollow tree,
when Sarah whispered, "Look!"

They were going back
to the hollow tree,
when Sarah said, "Look!"

Mr Gotobed was still sitting propped up
against the bench, fast asleep.
His hat was tilted over his eyes,
and Peter's mouse was sitting
on top of his hat!

The mouse was sitting
on Mr Gotobed's hat!

Peter was going to run forward,
but Sarah caught his arm.
"Sh!" she said. "Don't frighten her.
Let Davy do it.
He's good with mice."

"Let Davy get the mouse,"
said Sarah.

Davy tiptoed over to Mr Gotobed.
He held out his hand.
A nut was lying on his fingers.
The little mouse saw the nut.
Davy put his hand very close
to the hat, and the little mouse
climbed onto his hand
to eat the nut.

The little mouse
saw the nut.
She began to eat it.

Davy gently carried the mouse
back to Peter.

"Here you are, Peter," he said.

"Let's put her back in the cage,"
said Peter.

"It's a very small cage," said Sarah.

"Uncle Percy's getting me
a bigger one," said Peter.

Davy took the mouse
back to Peter Puffle.

They had just put the little mouse
back in the cage, when
Mr Puffle came into the garden.
"Hello, Sarah, Davy," said Mr Puffle.
"Have you got that dry grass, Peter?"

"I've got lots of it," said Peter.

"Good," said Mr Puffle. "I've got
a much bigger cage for your mouse.
And I've got another mouse,
to be with her,
so that she won't be lonely.
Bring the mouse along, and we'll put
her in her new home."

Mr Puffle came
into the garden.

So Sarah, Davy, Peter and the mouse
all went back into Puddle Lane,
to put Peter's mouse
in her new home.

They all went back
to Puddle Lane
with the little white mouse.

## Notes for the parent/teacher

Turn back to the beginning, and print the child's name in the space on the title page, using ordinary, not capital letters.

Now go through the book again. Look at each picture and talk about it. Point to the caption below, and read it aloud yourself.

Run your finger along under the words as you read, so that the child learns that reading goes from left to right.

Encourage the child to read the words under the illustrations. Don't rush in with the word before he/she has had time to think, but don't leave him/her struggling.

Read this story as often as the child likes hearing it. The more opportunities he/she has of looking at the illustrations and **reading** the captions with you, the more he/she will come to recognise the words.

If you have several books, let the child choose which story he/she would like.

"No. ...
"I live in the Map
at the end of Puddle Lane.
But I always come here on Fridays.
They have cheese and nuts
in the market on Fridays.
Come and see."

Jeremy looked down.
He looked at one of the tables.
There was a big cheese
at one end of the table,
and a basket of nuts
at the other end.

Jeremy looked down.

17